LEW WATANABE

Master of Stone and Light

by Kathy Childs
with Del Weston

Photography by Del Weston, Ronan Spelman, and Elena Rogovsky; Anthony Miele, Photography Assistant
Written by Kathy Childs with Del Weston
Layout Design by Jennifer Boeshore
Project Coordinator: Theresa Coscarelli
Photo manipulation by Ronan Spelman
Production Assistant: Aaron Green

www.efcfilm.com
www.lewwatanabe.com

ISBN: 1-59975-128-3

Printed in the United States of America.

DEDICATION

Private Collection
Sierra Madre, California

We dedicate this book to Lew's continued healing process. Lew was injured while creating one of his beautiful environments. His doctors, therapists and volunteers have worked tirelessly to assist him in regaining his health. Lew has moved from being bed-ridden to wheel-chair charged.

With the proceeds of this book going to the fund created for his medical expenses, Lew will be able to obtain additional professional help.

The photos in this book are amazing. These images are incredible pieces of art taken by some very talented photographers who have worked with Del Weston of EFC Productions to bring Lew's visions to the printed page. The editors, artists and people who believe in Lew have come together in an effort to support our friend.

Lew Watanabe is a phenomenal artist. The world of plants, stones, water and nature are his pallet. All the pictures you see in this book are his works of landscaping and art and they include monoliths, waterfalls, koi ponds, sculptures, and the creation of peaceful and serene environments.

I would like to personally thank you all for your involvement. From the bottom of our hearts, the "Book Team", dedicates this book to Lew Watanabe.

Kathy Childs

BIO
GRAPHY

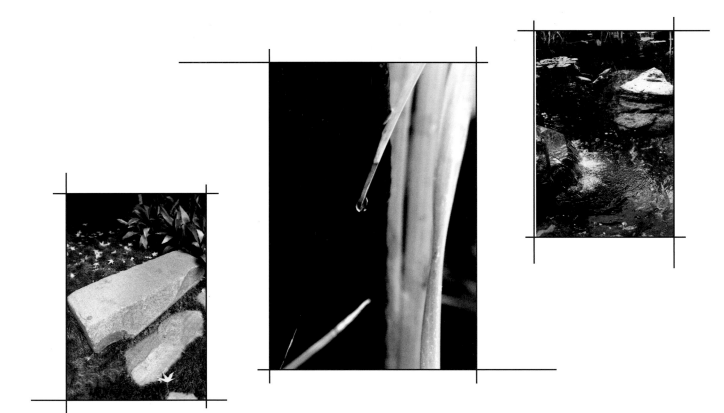

Lew Watanabe

"Lew Watanabe was born Dec. 1st, 1933 in Ogden Utah, the seventh of nine children born to Seizo and Konami (Kikuchi) Watanabe, who immigrated from Sendai, Japan to Hawaii in the late 1800's. They moved to Idaho and later settled on a farm in Utah.

Lew attended school in Utah graduating from Davis High in Kaysville in 1953. After serving three years in the U.S. Army, Lew moved his mother, younger brother and sister to Azusa, California.

Lew worked at a nursery in Azusa while attending night classes at Citrus College and the Los Angeles Arboretum, to learn more about the plants he was dealing with. His experience grew while working in the Retail Nursery business in Pasadena. Lew later found employment at a wholesale bedding plant company, where he met his bride-to-be who was working at a San Marnio Nursery.

The artist, his wife Joyce and his newly acquired family Randy and Steve Sage moved to Sierra Madre in 1965. He had often visited friends who lived there and had a desire to live in what he called "a great little town." In a 1998 interview, Lew stated that moving to Sierra Madre "was like coming home".

In his community everyone knows Lew or has been touched by him. His willingness to volunteer to help in beautifying his neighborhood - which includes the entire town - is well known and appreciated. This is, perhaps, the reason so many people came to his aid when he had the terrible accident which paralyzed him and almost took his life. He survived only because two men on the job site knew CPR.

In a town well known for its' volunteerism, people came together in astounding ways to help Lew recover; sitting with him at the hospital, bringing him tasty tidbits from the 'outside world', as well as moving his hands, arms and legs to keep the muscles from atrophying. His friends also sent cards to encourage him and brought plants and flowers to cheer him. They also brought dinner every night for months. Even today, his friends continue to help with physical therapy which provides the stretching he needs to keep his body going until it is able to work on its own.

With his inner sense of beauty and commitment to nature, he has designed tranquil and serene environments that invite all to enjoy. And even as he recovers from his fall he, with the capable assistance of his foreman, Ubaldo "Arturo" Garcia, continue to create remarkable landscapes and place his Water Sculptures with the eye of a true master of stone and light."

Joyce Watanabe

4

"Lew Watanabe's site specific sculptures deal with an encompassing visual and tactile experience. He conceives each piece of his art as a landscape, dealing with open sky, light, plants, and stone. The act of placing the sculpture heightens the appreciation of the art itself and creates an amalgamation with nature.

In 1987, Watanabe began designing and building his granite weeping water walls and was immediately praised for his ability to create meditative pieces that inspire reflection and serenity."

Lois Neiter, Agent

Private Collection
Sierra Madre, California

AWARDS

- Citizen of the Year, City of Sierra Madre, California
- "Fine Garden" Magazine Award
- Theme Award, Los Angeles, State and County Arboretum Garden Show
- Rose Marie Head Award, Los Angeles State and County Arboretum
- First Prize, Los Angeles State and County Arboretum Garden Show

EXHIBITIONS

- Carl Schlosberg Fine Arts, Sherman Oaks, California
- Malibu International Sculpture Exhibition
- Lois Neiter Fine Arts, Sherman Oaks, California
- Carl Schlosberg Fine Arts, Sherman Oaks, California
- Barnsdall Art Park, Los Angeles, California
  "Elements" – "In the Beginning" – Earth Elegies II"
  in collaboration with D. Paul/ Small

- 1997 Lois Neiter Fine Arts, Sherman Oaks, California
- 1997 Carl Schlosberg Fine Arts, Sherman Oaks, California
- 1996 Lois Neiter Fine Arts, Sherman Oaks, California
- 1996 Carl Schlosberg Fine Arts, Malibu, California
- 1995 Lois Neiter Fine Arts, Sherman Oaks, California
- 1995 Carl Schlosberg Fine Arts, Sherman Oaks, California
- 1994 Lois Neiter Fine Arts, Sherman Oaks, California
- 1994 Carl Schlosberg Fine Arts, Sherman Oaks, California
- 1993 Malibu International Sculpture Exhibition, Malibu, California
- 1993 Lois Neiter Fine Arts, Sherman Oaks, California
- 1992 Lois Neiter Fine Arts, Sherman Oaks, California
- 1991 Lois Neiter Fine Arts, Sherman Oaks, California

PUBLIC COLLECTIONS
- Descanso Gardens – Two untitled Memorial Benches
- 2001 Proposed: U.C.L.A. Medical Center
- 2000 Pepperdine University,
  Frederick Weisman Museum Sculpture Park (April)
- 1999 "Weeping Wall Memorial",
  Memorial Park, City of Sierra Madre, California
- 1999 Untitled Monolith,
  Descanso Gardens, La Canada, California
- 1999 Japanese Pavilion and Garden,
  Descanso Gardens, La Canada, California
- 1998 "Weeping Wall" and Bench,
  Descanso Gardens, La Canada, California
- 1997 "Silent Song" – Malibu Sculpture Park
  at Cross Creek, Malibu, California
- 1996 Untitled Benches,
  Stephen S. Wise Temple, Los Angeles, California
- 1995 Japanese Garden,
  Sierra Madre Elementary School, Sierra Madre, California
- 1994 "Tranquility" – Valley Beth Shalom, Encino, California

ARTICLES
- "Watanabe" – Sierra Madre Weekly, February 10, 1999
- "Park Wall" – Pasadena Star-News, April 14, 1999
- "Wall Dedicated" – Sierra Madre Weekly, April 28, 1999
- "Weeping Wall" – Sierra Madre Weekly, May 5, 1999
- "Weeping Wall" – Sierra Madre Mountain Views,
  May 7, 1999
- "Serenity Restored" – San Gabriel Valley Weekly,
  March 20, 1998
- "The Art of Gardening" – Valley Magazine, July, 1998
- "Living Lesson" – The Rafu Shimpo, February 5, 1997
- "Healing the Wounds of War" – Koi, USA, July 8, 1997
- "Art in the Afternoon" – Malibu Times,
  December 4, 1997
- "Friendship Gesture" – Star-News, January 4, 1996
- "Citizen Beautifies Area" – Herald Tribune,
  January 18, 1996
- "Inspired by Nature" – Voices, Home and Garden,
  February 2, 1996
- "Local Treasure" – Star-News, February 13, 1996
- "Vandals Attack Friendship..." – Herald Tribune,
  June 14, 1996
- "Artist and Ambassador" – Sierra Madre News,
  July 11, 1996
- "Goodwill Gesture" – Los Angeles Times,
  August 24, 1996
- "Japanese Garden" – Sierra Madre News,
  August 24, 1996
- "Treasure of Sierra Madre" – Sierra Madre News,
  January 26, 1995
- "Japanese Garden" – Sierra Madre News,
  August 24, 1995
- "Work of Art" – San Gabriel News, March 3, 1994
- "Artist Combines Skills to Create Tranquil Places"
  Los Angeles Times, January 4, 1991

Private Collection
Hollywood, California

Right: Descanso Gardens
La Cañada, California

Left: Private Collection
Sierra Madre, California

8

LANDSCAPE

Private Collection
Sierra Madre, California

Lew does not consider his landscape work to be a job. Once he arrived at this conclusion he was able to dedicate himself to the practice of creating the perfect spaces, gardens and yards based on the challenges and limitations each property presents.

The work begins with an initial 'meet' with the clients to discuss their mutual ideas and needs. Once a conceptual design is created and an agreement of what will and what will not work in the environment is reached, the project has a starting point. From that point, Lew considers the property his own and he moves forward with his mission to create the best possible outcome.

Not only does the artist use stone, water, plants and trees in his quest for perfection, he also takes into account the natural gifts each location provides.

In every case, home, office, park, school or public space, Lew strives for beauty, balance and peace which are the hallmarks of a signature Watanabe project.

The Los Angeles County Arboretum was home to this weeping water piece and signature bench with complimentary landscape. This is an example of one of Lew's temporary installations.

The sun shines through the trees illuminating Lew's beautiful work.

Private Collection
Arcadia, California

Harsh shadows are made delicate and balance is restored in this very inviting backyard.

Private Collection
Sierra Madre, California

The stairway leads to serenity, peace and quite rest.

14

Nature shines in areas beautifully outlined in stone and plant life.

Left: Descanso Gardens
Sierra Madre, California

Right: Private Collection
San Marino, California

"Lew Watanabe's work takes one past excellence and into the real sense of peace, tranquility, and elevation; all of which are the transcendent values of traditional Japanese gardens and landscapes. Our 'Watanabe Gardens' were begun over fifteen years ago. With little maintenance they have only mellowed with time. We continue to add new elements with Lew and feel even more 'elated' with each addition."

Roy Aaron

"Strength, balance, sight, and sound - beauty here is all around."

Left and Right: Private Collections
Los Angeles, California

"We have had the pleasure of working with Lew Watanabe on our landscaping for twelve years and our lawn and gardens reflect his artistic design capabilities. In addition to his artistry and knowledge, Lew is always open to suggestions, considerate, kind, efficient and reliable. We're very proud of our landscaping - a labor of love - thanks to Lew and his team!"

Wayne & Karen Whitehill

Top: Private Collection
Sierra Madre, California

Opposite: Private Collection
Hollywood, California

Bottom: Private Collection
Arcadia, California

The artist, working on a bonzai tree
early in his career

"Using natural elements, Lew developed the aesthetic potential of our garden. We learned to trust Lew's suggestions as he worked his magic to transform our garden into a serene, peaceful haven. We look forward to the changing colors of the Japanese maples and ginkgo trees, and the flowering of the azaleas, camellias, cherry trees and wisteria.

Joan Kobori & Elliot Meyerowitz

This magnificent tree was chosen to balance the look of his client's yard.

"Lew Watanabe is a master of sculpture and master of natural design. His work offers serenity in this busy world."

Edith Fischer

Private Collection
Arcadia, California

Opposite: Private Collection
Beverly Hills, California

Top: Private Collection
Arcadia, California

Right: Private Collection
Sierra Madre, California

Private Collection
Arcadia, California

"A beautiful landscape from a beautiful friend."

Gary Fidone

Private Collection
Los Angeles, California

Private Collection
Los Angeles, California

Top: Private Collection
Sierra Madre, California

Right: Private Collection
Sierra Madre, California

Private Collection
Arcadia, California

Private Collection
Los Angeles, California

Private Collection
Sierra Madre, California

Left: Private Collection
Pacific Palisades

42

Right: Private Collections
Los Angeles, California

43

Top: Private Collection
Sierra Madre, California

Right: Private Collection
San Marino, California

Private Collection
Los Angeles, California

Left & Right: Private Collections
Los Angeles, California

WATER

Watanabe is cognizant of the role water plays in both the beauty of the garden and the psychological impact it has on his clients. Water gardens and pool designs usually represent a stand-alone art form. Lew has a respect for nature and reliance on his own sensibilities, and is able to assemble many minor elements into one cohesive artistic picture using pools, sculptures, weeping walls, plants and light.

The Japanese gardens were specifically designed to promote a balance of nature and harmony where quiet meditation and tranquility could be achieved.

For thousands of years, the garden with the shimmer, sparkle and shine of water has provided peaceful environments often times with a sense of great religious and almost mystical significance. Every culture throughout the ages has adopted the art of gardening and landscaping with water.

When visiting a water garden, it is easy to understand that the reason for its creation was beauty, nature and serenity. A peaceful environment created especially for relaxation can be found in the soothing, calming surroundings of a water garden. Architects have been hired for centuries to design meditative gardens where every visitor could find peace and tranquility. The Japanese gardens were specifically designed to promote a balance of nature and harmony where quiet meditation and tranquility could be achieved.

Japanese gardeners and architects have devised methods throughout the ages of creating natural landscapes that are a reduction of some aspect of the natural whole world; as an example, they create rocks to display mountains while building a small pond to give the impression of a much larger body of water. The simplification of a complex balance of nature is an art that involves both the creator as well as the observer of the garden.

Knowing this and living with his natural talent for design, Lew creates his garden environments to incorporate plants, stones, water and animal life. His use of the leafy Japanese maples as overhead cover and color is quite by design. His use of stones, water, and plants, create a beautiful, natural appearance. Lew designs his settings to appear as if Mother Nature herself had placed all of the elements used in a particular environment.

The landscaped garden is not shut out or removed from the rest of the area; it is incorporated into the environment but still provides privacy for meditation and contemplation.

Stones in the Japanese gardens have been in the form of lanterns, artifacts, bridges, basins and accents. Lew took the use of stone to a new level by incorporating the stone into the garden and having it weep. He plumbs the water up through the stone and creates a soft overflow of water over the piece causing it to appear to sparkle and shine as the

water moves over the surface. The effect is perfect for both small private areas and larger garden areas such as public parks. The sound is soft, gentle and soothing. In addition, Lew provides stone benches; simply placed in an area that is conducive to meditation.

As an artist, Lew has been able to incorporate the art of Japanese gardening and landscaping with the California environment. The creation of a meditative haven has been an evolution for Lew. His creativity has always provided his gardens with a style that balances and combines natural locations and man made structures to create the tranquil settings his clients desire.

Lew was always concerned about our visiting his gardens that had not been maintained to his exacting standards. However, as we toured the gardens we found that even the locations that were not perfectly maintained, were absolutely beautiful. The integration of all of the elements used by the artist seem to continually evolve and while maybe not perfect in his eyes, they are certainly perfect as they grow and mature into their own timeless beauty.

Private Collection
Sierra Madre, California

*This is an excellent
example of Watanabe's
use of multiple elements
to bring about one
cohesive and perfectly
matched landscape.*

Private Collection
San Marino, California

This photo is of a Japanese water basin known as a tsukubai, a bowl that historically allowed a visitor to refresh themselves and to wash their hands before taking tea.

Quite a few traditional Japanese gardens have these beautiful tsukubai basins incorporated into their gardens, but many people are not aware of their significance or history. Because of the sound of the water and its inspiring beauty, this vessel is popular in Japanese gardens and is used frequently for accents and in some cases such as this, as a focal point because of its strong visual impact.

Bamboo is also frequently used with such pieces. This plant is very durable and if unchecked, will quietly take over a yard or entire area. In order to maintain control of the sprouting bamboo, many gardeners will place them in pots to decorate a garden, a border of a garden or behind glass as an added dimension of greenery.

Once cut, bamboo will last for a long time; it is a very sturdy and beautiful addition to gardens, ponds, and obviously tsukubai basins. This particular basin is part of an incredibly powerful yet understated garden created by Lew Watanabe.

Private Collection
Sherman Oaks, California

"Lew is the perfect combination of artisan and craftsman."

Gayle Bluemel

Private Collection
Sierra Madre, California

61

Private Collection
Lois Neiter

Private Collections
Sierra Madre, California

"Not a day goes by that I don't look out of our window and admire our beautiful Lew Watanabe water piece. It adds so much to our landscaping. A simple and beautiful Zen feeling in a very difficult to landscape area. We love it so much!"

Kelly Lynch

Every element in this piece is used to create a stunning effect from any angle. Lew is a master of contrasts.

Private Collection
Sierra Madre, California

Balance is achieved easily between the harsh weight of the stone and delicate beauty of the Maples that accent it.

The original landscape was dry and bland, but with a few strokes of his brush Watanabe was able to bring beauty, light and drama.

Original photo taken during the creation of the Sierra Madre School's Goodwill Garden

Sierra Madre School
yet another treasure

The story of the Sierra Madre School was not complete until Lew took on the task of rebuilding the environment after many years of vandalism and decay.

Lew's efforts created a wonderful gift to the community and to all of the children who enjoy this incredible water feature.

Students discovered the garden buried under rubble.

SCULPTURE

For his incredible sculptures Lew visits a rock quarry where he makes his way around the entire area studying each and every stone. He studies the angles, the size, the scope and the way each stone fits into the earth. He notes the color, shape and dimensions then lets his mind wander to imagine the end result of how this stone will be used in his work.

Knowing the layout of the property where the stone will be utilized and placed is only a small part of his entire process. How a stone will be sculpted and how water will look moving over its surface is also considered. The number and types of plants to be used and how they are to be placed is brought into his equation. All of this is part of the artist's visualization process.

Watanabe never puts plan to paper, rather he works from his imagination, his intuition and with a very unique vision of his own ultimate masterpiece.

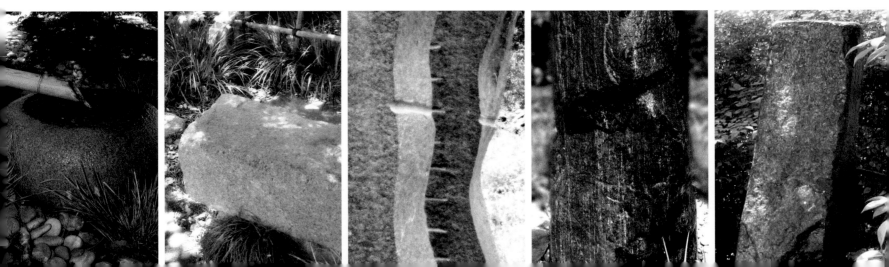

"Lew's beautiful stone sculpture was a 50th anniversary present to ourselves. It's planted in the midst of our garden and we love seeing the water falling over the stones."
Mark and Peachy Levy

The Weeping Wall

"The quiet and sometimes silent passing of water over stone resembles the stone actually weeping..." Those were the words of Joyce Watanabe, the person credited with naming the pieces for which Lew is most well known.

In Sierra Madre the "Weeping Wall" is placed in the center of town, in Memorial Park, to honor veterans of the community, but there are many more walls in private collections around the country.

Of his creation, Lew said, "In the spring of 1987, I had a bunch of granite piled up in my backyard and I wanted to do something different." That one thought led Lew to create his fantastic stone monoliths that have taken him from his backyard on a journey to famous places. Lew's granite, water, sunlight, blue skies and peaceful surroundings combine to create the trademark of this magnificent artistry.

The black mass of granite, pulled from a quarry and sculpted into a place of serenity is an extension of Lew's dreams and visions. The granite mass is sculpted by the artist. The most popular stones in his creations are made from African granite and mahogany granite.

In addition to the stone sculptures, Lew artfully uses plants that are in his opinion, 'suitable to the environment'. He places the plants around the base of his sculptures and his weeping walls. Many clients have requested that Lew place his custom stone benches near the pieces in order to create spaces that can be used for contemplation, meditation or just to enjoy the beauty of the artist's work.

Lew's skills come from a combination of his Japanese-American heritage and sensibilities, his natural talents and his expertise as a gardener and landscape artist. Not only does he use the environment, he uses all of the elements from the sky to the earth in the careful placement of each piece.

Due to his innovative method of not using plans or blueprints, clients of the artist are free to make suggestions, give criticism or interject their ideas throughout his creative process. Lew simply incorporates their ideas and works with both his ideas and those of his clients to create the perfect piece.

Lew's agent Lois Neiter has his work in her home and gallery. When interviewed by writer Karen Dardick in 1996, Neiter said, "There's something very special about Lew's work. He creates site-specific art evoking such peace and tranquility that visitors keep returning to view them." Lois also added, "Lew conceives each piece of his art as a landscape, not as an artificial object on site. He creates a totality of experience as each part of the landscape is interrelated to open sky, light, plants, stone and scale." Lew entered Lois's life during a time when she was ill and she still says that she does not know what she would have done without him. Lois says, "He, [Lew] took a personal interest in me and helped me heal." Lois and her husband Richard have a deep love and respect for Lew and Lois is very much a part of Lew's growth in the industry.

Lew began to create his walls originally at his Wildomar ranch by shaping granite sculptures using a chisel on the stone. Once the pattern was created, he adds a water movement system and his magnificent weeping walls were created. It sounds simple but anyone who has ever seen the walls or seen Lew work can tell you that it is anything but simple.

Lew loves the strength of the rock and the masculine statement the pieces make but he ads the beauty of plants and water to soften the stone and to create a balance in the environment. The visual effect of the work is stunning, and the addition of the sound and accents the water creates, combine to result in the peaceful and tranquil feelings that are universal to all who have experienced the work.

One of Lew's clients contacted and retained him because of his calm and self assured manner. She said, "Everyone else was so clinical with specific plans that seemed ordinary...Lew was different. He really treated it like an artist." She went on to say, "When you enter the space that Lew transformed, you are transformed. Lew's environments can stop you in your tracks, take away your cares and allow you to think, meditate and enjoy the garden."

Having been to Lois Neiter's home and having seen a number of Lew's pieces in person, I can tell you, I understand that sense, that feeling.

Lois Neiter once told me, "One of my friends says that when she closes her eyes, wherever she is, and tries to create a peaceful, meditative feeling, she pictures Lew's weeping wall in my yard. It's very powerful."

Private Collections
Van Nuys, California

Left: Arch from
Descanso Gardens

Top: Private Collection
Hollywood, California

Private Collection
Pacific Palisades, California

Private Collections
Hollywood, California

Private Collection
Van Nuys, California

"Lew's stone monolith, which we chose as a memorial for our son Mark, is the focal point of our tranquil sculpture garden. The many birds, which visit, enjoy their baths on top of the piece and it gives great pleasure to all who enter our garden. Not a day goes by that I don't look out the window and admire our beautiful water sculpture. We love it so much!"

Elaine Freund

"Our visitors all admire our gardens, designed by Lew Watanabe. His work continues to inspire us and we enjoy our gardens year around."
Angel Unamuno

Private Collections
Hollywood and Los Angeles, California

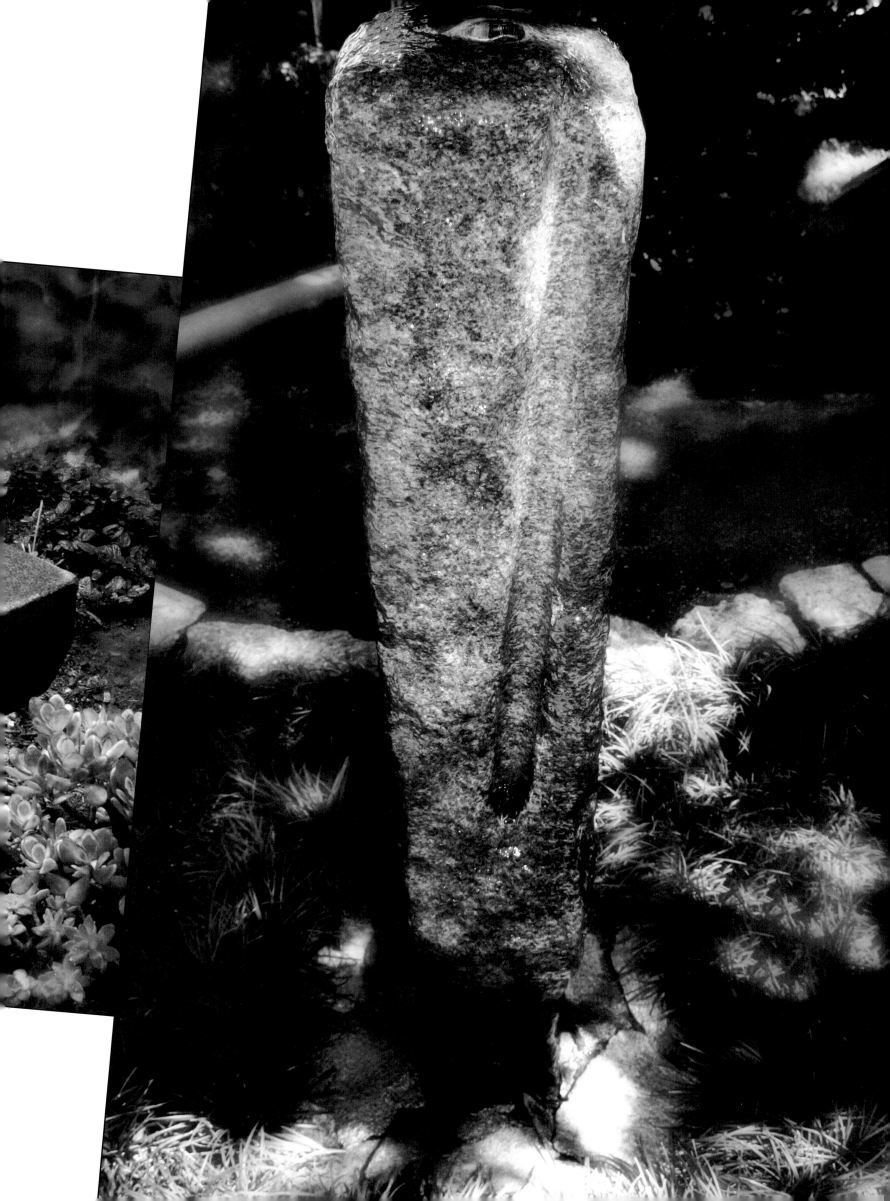

"Lew Watanabe has an eye for possibilities. He can take an idea and create a design that delights. The fountain and ponds were designed by Don Hornbeck of Don Hornbeck and Associates, built and landscaped by Lew Watanabe."

Janice M. Speery

Private Collections
Sierra Madre, California

Private Collection
Pacific Palisades, California

Private Collection
Sierra Madre, California

Private Collection
Los Angeles, California

Left: Private Collection
Sierra Madre, California

"By day, Lew Watanabe's sculpture is a monolith whose cool, cascading water softly beckons to both birds and people alike.

As day becomes night, so too does the fountain transform. The up-lights surrounding the stone sculpture casts a golden, hypnotic aura upon it.

Thank you Lew for your art, your integrity, and for your artistic courage."
-Alexander & Judith Angerman

"Lew created a sanctuary
for us. A spot to relax and
contemplate nature. The
heart of this refuge is the
beautiful weeping stone we
chose to call 'My Serenity'.
Bless you, Lew"
John and Grace O'Brien

"Lew's work inspires and nurtures the spirit in all who have an opportunity to experience it."
Lois Neiter

Private Collections
Van Nuys and Los Angeles, California

Private Collection
Van Nuys, California

"Lew's design respected the woodland setting of the canyon. The design looks like a natural evolution of the surrounding landscape. The dry streambed suggests the flow of water in a naturally dry environment."

Jay and Donna Packer

Private Collections
Sierra Madre and Los Angeles, California

"The first Watanabe, Barry and I purchased was the granite monolith water feature installed in our upper meadow. We saw it at a spring art exhibit at Carl Schlosberg's, on his front lawn; it was the first piece to greet us upon our arrival, and we agonized about the stone bench in front of it, we wanted it as well but talked ourselves out of it. The subsequent installation in our meadow was exciting and although not easy, Lew prepared well for it so it went "like silk". The day of installation was to be my first meeting with Lew, and we liked each other right away. This first piece is an interactive one with nature, catching the morning light on its watery face, inviting both human touch and our dogs' tongues; birds like it too, stopping to rest on its vertical perch. The installation included landscaping, so Lew's stone "grows", not from hardscape but from river rock, black mondo and liriope, backed by the lacy curtain of a Japanese maple selected by the artist.

The second Watanabe installation would be several years later, and an ambitious one for us. We asked Lew to design a pond for us, with pathway and bridge. I showed Lew several pictures of what we had in mind and then we waited with great anticipation. When it was nearly complete, Lew started talking to me about koi...and I was very dubious, not welcoming more complications in our lives. "Well of course you've got to have fish! You can't have water and no fish!" was Lew's reaction. His logic sounded so absolute and sound, we never thought to question it. The koi came into our lives, along with great joy and pleasure to see their glistening bodies in the dappled water. Waterlilies were added bringing dragonflies to our new place. This provided a beautiful spot for morning coffee and evening wine. The waterfall diffused the busy traffic sounds, and the new evening lights brought another dimension to the garden at night. We cannot imagine how we ever lived here without the pond! As I write this, the Ginkgo leaves are starting to change and soon their reflection in the pond will change to molten gold.

As for our newest Watanabe addition...that one is actually an old one that was waiting many years to come here. The granite bench we saw long ago at Carl's

113

is finally where it belongs. Lew and Arturo installed it on a path in our garden with woolly thyme and succulents where it gives us all a much needed spot to rest and contemplate our good fortune. The stone is still warm from the sun even as twilight brings its chill. From Lew's bench, I can see the iceberg roses in the fading light, and enjoy the last blooms of the crape myrtle on the hillside. A trug filled daisies and roses I cut for the house rests next to me on this, Lew's Bench."

Margaret Kemp

"His piece of sculpture standing in full view from our breakfast room lends a pure design presence to our immediate environment and the circulating water conjures thoughts of fresh springtime. We have enjoyed it immensely for years!"
                                                                                    Sandy Gaynor

"*We are very pleased with the water sculptures that Lew Watanabe designed for us. Not only are they beautiful and enhance the property, the fountains also are a source of pleasure for many birds, squirrels and our ten year old grandson.*"

Beverly Gladstone

117

"Lew Watanabe must hold an image of beauty within him. He came into our garden and transformed the landscape.

Lew found an old stone in the yard and upended it to make it art. Then he made the stone a fountain where hummingbirds come to bathe.

Lew highlighted the on-going life of the garden with an array of Japanese maples which lose their leaves in fall to return green shoots in spring. Other plants he organized in a way that invited a sense of peace. Lew brought to our garden the mystery of art and with his touch an inscrutable essence of the inscrutable East. We are deeply appreciative."

Jack & Maude Ann Taylor

Top: Private Collection
Los Angeles, California

Private Collection
Sierra Madre, California

"Our Lew Watanabe Japanese Garden has provided
endless pleasure with its tranquil beauty designed
with a perfect balanced interplay of water, rock,
lanterns, black pine, bamboo and colorful oriental
trees, plants and grasses.

It was remarkable how Lew constructed
the garden with its dry river bed, granite
water basin fed by a bamboo pipe, varied
oriental trees, plants and grasses with a
traditional Japanese gate; all without a
visible plan as the painting artist would
create their image without an outline.
Lew is truly a remarkable creative artist."
Dr. & Mrs. Robert P. Natelson

Private Collections
Hollywood and Los Angeles, California

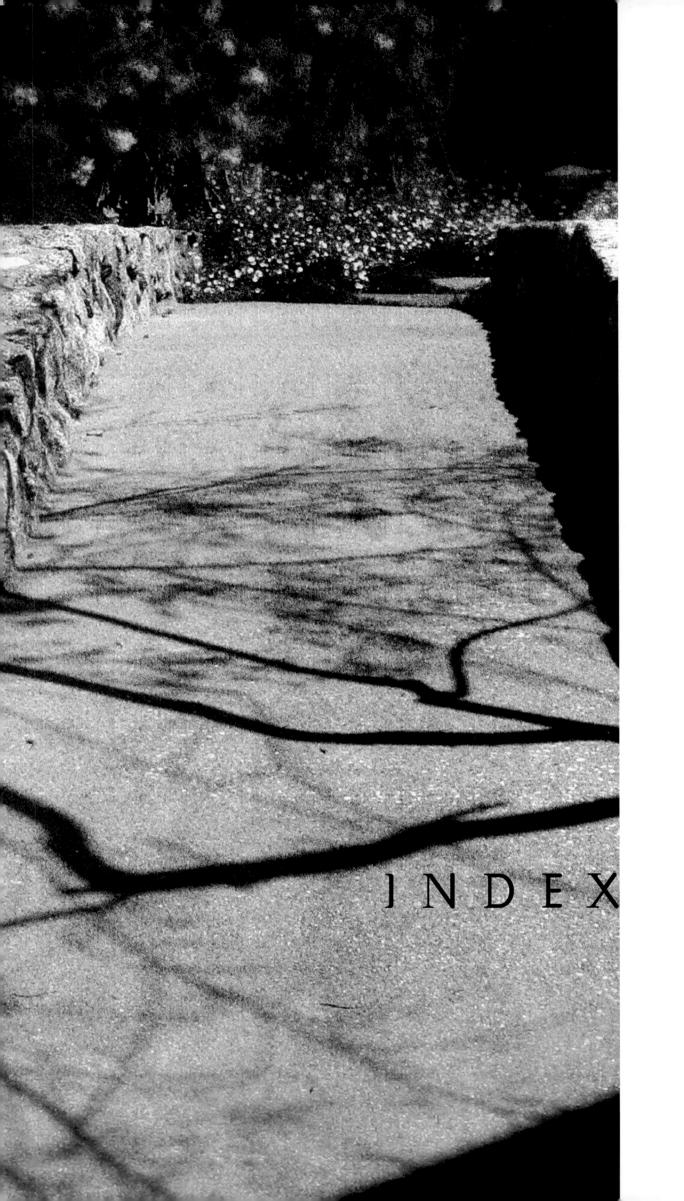

INDEX

Kathy Childs...is a woman who wrote a book for a friend. Samples of her work can be seen cover to cover.

Del Weston...is a writer, artist and producer who has worked on projects for a number of clients involved in film, video, graphics and of course fine art. Weston looks for projects that inspire him to challenge not only his abilities but his understanding and beliefs about art. His upcoming projects include two new films and a book of poetry that blends striking graphic images with words of wisdom and change.

"As good as we think we might be, there is always something or someone who can make our work better. I am constantly on the lookout for that person or that thing. In this process, Kathy Childs was the person and Lew Watanabe's work was the thing. Thanks to you both."

Samples of Del's photography can be found on the following pages:
2, 5, 10, 13, 22, 23-24, 29, 30, 34, 35, 41, 42, 45-46, 48, 52, 69, 70, 71, 71-72, 73, 74, 75-76, 78, 80, 86, 93, 96, 97, 104, 113, 114, 115, 116, 119, 120, 127-128, 132.

Ronan Spelman, born in Dublin, Ireland, studied art, design, & media studies at the National College of Art and Design, "N.C.A.D.", Ireland. Now living in Los Angles as an established digital artist, Ronan has had many solo and group shows in Ireland, England, Los Angeles, and Chicago. He brings much of his formal fine art training into his work as a photographer with his use of color and composition and techniques.

"I truly feel that I owe my art and love of art to my father and late mother, Mary. Both encouraged me in my endeavors and my struggles. Also to my friends, my son, Kyle, and Lourdes who have stood by me and kept me on the path when times were tough. To all of you I am very grateful, and I thank you from the bottom of my heart."

Samples of Ronan's photography can be found on the following pages:
8, 9, 10, 14, 15, 17, 19, 20, 21, 26, 31-32, 33, 35, 36, 37, 38, 39, 40, 42, 44, 43, 47, 49, 50, 53, 54, 57, 58, 59, 60, 61, 62, 65-66, 67, 68, 77, 78, 81, 83, 84, 88, 89, 90, 99, 100, 103, 104, 105, 109, 110, 111, 112, 117, 118, 121, 123, 124, 129, 131.

Elena Rogovsky a native of Kiev, Ukraine, grew up living in Israel, South Africa, and Canada while nurturing her developing love of photography. Capturing her life memories through a lens before her family's next inevitable move. She has demonstrated a unique world-view perspective of her immediate surroundings. As a adult, she continues traveling on her own, having recently completed exploring and photographing throughout central and western Europe and the South Pacific. She now lives in Los Angeles full time, working in motion films and as a still photographer.

Samples of Elena's photography can be found on the following pages:
1, 3, 6, 7, 11-12, 16, 18, 25, 27-28, 51, 55-56, 63-64, 78, 79, 85, 91, 92, 95, 98, 101-102, 107, 108-109, 122, 125-126.

Jennifer Boeshore is an artist of unusual talent, integrity and power. She was born in Southern California, and has a sophisticated air but the integrity of someone who comes from quality and maintains it in all of her work. She possesses the uncanny ability to develop concepts and ideas with very little input from the client. 'She just knows what to do.' Her style is in stark contrast to what you would expect from a young artist because it has such weight and gravity, it also has an element of experience that younger artists working today just don't possess. She has a very unique vision when it comes to layout, text, design, color and how they all work together. Her complete ability to visualize what works and what doesn't and then to convey those ideas to everyone else, really makes her invaluable as a designer. This is her first major book, but it won't be her last.

A number of other artists and designers have worked on this project, we would like to thank them as well.

"Our special thanks to all our clients who contributed to this book; to Del Weston for his enthusiasm and patience; and our deepest gratitude to Kathy Childs whose generosity and hard work made this book possible."

Lew Watanabe

We would like to thank the following families and individuals for their generous assistance in the creation of this book.

The Aarons

The Amstutzs

The Angermans

The Atkins'

The Beggs

G. Bluemel

The Burns

The Campbells

City of Sierra Madre

Cross Creek Shopping Center

G. Fidone

E. Fischer

E. Freund

The Gaynors

B. Gladstone

The Kemps

Kobori & Meyerowitz

The Kwons

The Levys

Kelly Lynch

Malibu Racquet Club

Memorial Park

The Natelsons

Lois Neiter

The O'Briens

The Olsons

The Packers

Sierra Madre Elementary School

The Shapiros

J.M. Speery

The Smiths

The Taylors

The Unamunos

The Whitehills

I thank you all...

Lew and Joyce, thank you for your time, for reviewing thousands of pictures and for your patience as we worked to succeed in putting your pictures before the public to admire.

Lois Neiter, your eye for art, your determination to put Lew's art "out there" and your undying devotion to the art world gives me a true sense of pride to have met you. Your comments and history and selfless giving of your time and effort made this book possible. Thank you.

Ria Richie, of Creative Framing, I thank you for framing the works of art in a manner that is so impressive, professional, beautiful and pleasing to everyone involved. The donation of your framing, your time and skill is beyond what I can thank you for.

Gil and Michelle and the staff at Restaurant Lozano in Sierra Madre, thank you for the use of your amazing restaurant for our art show and the book signing. Your calm and positive attitude and continued support of this project is truly appreciated by our entire team. Thank you.

Ernie Camacho of Pacifica Services, Inc., my friend and boss, thank you for letting me use the copier in the evenings and occupy the office on Sundays...your belief in me and the project is a boost to the efforts I have enjoyed. Thank you.

The team at EFC with Del Weston! Thank you, thank you, thank you for the skill level, the over-time you put in, your eye for photographic excellence, your layout skills and editing made it all come together...thank you all!

My husband Charlie, my daughters, Andrea, Becky and Marianne...too many missed meals, missed evenings and weekends all so I could work on "the book". Thank you all for your love, support and encouragement. I love you all!

Kathy Childs

"Not only does Lew have excellent ideas in regard to design and plant material, but his crew does first class work. They are all a pleasure to work with."

Patti Amstutz

INDEX

Kathy Childs...is a woman who wrote a book for a friend. Samples of her work can be seen cover to cover.

Del Weston...is a writer, artist and producer who has worked on projects for a number of clients involved in film, video, graphics and of course fine art. Weston looks for projects that inspire him to challenge not only his abilities but his understanding and beliefs about art. His upcoming projects include two new films and a book of poetry that blends striking graphic images with words of wisdom and change.

"As good as we think we might be, there is always something or someone who can make our work better. I am constantly on the lookout for that person or that thing. In this process, Kathy Childs was the person and Lew Watanabe's work was the thing. Thanks to you both."

Samples of Del's photography can be found on the following pages:
2, 5, 10, 13, 22, 23-24, 29, 30, 34, 35, 41, 42, 45-46, 48, 52, 69, 70, 71, 71-72, 73, 74, 75-76, 78, 80, 86, 93, 96, 97, 104, 113, 114, 115, 116, 119, 120, 127-128, 132.

Ronan Spelman, born in Dublin, Ireland, studied art, design, & media studies at the National College of Art and Design, "N.C.A.D.", Ireland. Now living in Los Angles as an established digital artist, Ronan has had many solo and group shows in Ireland, England, Los Angeles, and Chicago. He brings much of his formal fine art training into his work as a photographer with his use of color and composition and techniques.

"I truly feel that I owe my art and love of art to my father and late mother, Mary. Both encouraged me in my endeavors and my struggles. Also to my friends, my son, Kyle, and Lourdes who have stood by me and kept me on the path when times were tough. To all of you I am very grateful, and I thank you from the bottom of my heart."

Samples of Ronan's photography can be found on the following pages:
8, 9, 10, 14, 15, 17, 19, 20, 21, 26, 31-32, 33, 35, 36, 37, 38, 39, 40, 42, 44, 43, 47, 49, 50, 53, 54, 57, 58, 59, 60, 61, 62, 65-66, 67, 68, 77, 78, 81, 83, 84, 88, 89, 90, 99, 100, 103, 104, 105, 109, 110, 111, 112, 117, 118, 121, 123, 124, 129, 131.

Elena Rogovsky a native of Kiev, Ukraine, grew up living in Israel, South Africa, and Canada while nurturing her developing love of photography. Capturing her life memories through a lens before her family's next inevitable move. She has demonstrated a unique world-view perspective of her immediate surroundings. As a adult, she continues traveling on her own, having recently completed exploring and photographing throughout central and western Europe and the South Pacific. She now lives in Los Angeles full time, working in motion films and as a still photographer.

Samples of Elena's photography can be found on the following pages:
1, 3, 6, 7, 11-12, 16, 18, 25, 27-28, 51, 55-56, 63-64, 78, 79, 85, 91, 92, 95, 98, 101-102, 107, 108-109, 122, 125-126.

Jennifer Boeshore is an artist of unusual talent, integrity and power. She was born in Southern California, and has a sophisticated air but the integrity of someone who comes from quality and maintains it in all of her work. She possesses the uncanny ability to develop concepts and ideas with very little input from the client. 'She just knows what to do.' Her style is in stark contrast to what you would expect from a young artist because it has such weight and gravity, it also has an element of experience that younger artists working today just don't possess. She has a very unique vision when it comes to layout, text, design, color and how they all work together. Her complete ability to visualize what works and what doesn't and then to convey those ideas to everyone else, really makes her invaluable as a designer. This is her first major book, but it won't be her last.

A number of other artists and designers have worked on this project, we would like to thank them as well.

"Our special thanks to all our clients who contributed to this book; to Del Weston for his enthusiasm and patience; and our deepest gratitude to Kathy Childs whose generosity and hard work made this book possible."

Lew Watanabe

We would like to thank the following families and individuals for their generous assistance in the creation of this book.

The Aarons
The Amstutzs
The Angermans
The Atkins'
The Beggs
G. Bluemel
The Burns
The Campbells
City of Sierra Madre
Cross Creek Shopping Center
G. Fidone
E. Fischer

E. Freund
The Gaynors
B. Gladstone
The Kemps
Kobori & Meyerowitz
The Kwons
The Levys
Kelly Lynch
Malibu Racquet Club
Memorial Park
The Natelsons
Lois Neiter

The O'Briens
The Olsons
The Packers
Sierra Madre Elementary School
The Shapiros
J.M. Speery
The Smiths
The Taylors
The Unamunos
The Whitehills